Christianity as a World Religion

CHRISTIAN BUILDINGS

Edited by **Brenda Lealman**

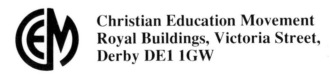
Christian Education Movement
Royal Buildings, Victoria Street,
Derby DE1 1GW

ABOUT CEM

The Christian Education Movement is a charitable foundation which, among other things, provides support for Religious Education in schools. It is funded partly by grants from local education authorities, and the Council of Local Education Authorities recommends its members to subscribe to CEM. Other sources of finance include grants from trusts and from the churches, and CEM also generates its own income through subscriptions and the sale of publications. It offers advisory services, runs conferences for both teachers and pupils, and provides higher quality resources for Regligious Education through its subscription services and publications catalogue. To receive further details, including the current catalogue, send to the address below.

Editor: Brenda Lealman

Contributors:

Patrick Bailey	– lecturer geography/education, University of Leicester
Vida Barnett	– former lecturer in higher education
Bill Greenwood	– former lecturer in higher education
Brenda Hoddinott	– RE teacher, Wheatley Park School, Oxford
Diana Houghton	– landscape architect and teacher
Reverend Michael Houghton	– priest, recently returned from St. Helena
Colin Johnson	– CEM Publications Officer
Brenda Lealman	– CEM/Westhill Fellow in RE Development
Angus Murdie	– student, Wheatley Park School, Oxford
Reverend Alan Payne	– Rector, Stanningley, Leeds
Reverend Sabaw Sinwa Naw	– Minister, Burma
Reverend John Sutcliffe	– Minister, URC Trinity Church, St. Albans

Acknowledgements:

Very many thanks go to the following people for their help and generous permission to use materials:

Prebendary M. W. Hooper, for permission to use material from *The Link* (November, 1989) the magazine for Leominster Team Ministry

Angus Murdie for line drawings on pages 25, 26, 28, 30, 32

Diana Houghton for all the other line drawings except where indicated

Many students at the Selly Oak Colleges, Birmingham, for their help

Front cover: The Church of the Resurrection at Orly, near Przemysl, Poland. Photographer: Edward Robinson
Back cover: Cross in New Road Baptist Church, Oxford. Sculptor: Heather Harms (1982). Photographer: Maurice Alden
Cross in Leominster Priory. Photographer: Colin Johnson

Series: Christianity as a World Religion
Series: 1. Christian Pilgrimage
Series: 2. Christian Buildings

ISBN 1 85100 009 7

Designed and printed by BPCC BLACKPOOL LTD., Stanley Road, Blackpool FY1 4QN

CONTENTS

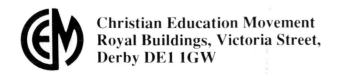

**Christian Education Movement
Royal Buildings, Victoria Street,
Derby DE1 1GW**

INTRODUCTION

This book is intended to stimulate interest in Christian buildings (not always simply "churches"), their uses and the people who use them. The book is in no way an exhaustive exploration of these topics but can be used as a guide by teachers wishing to develop a study within a local area; it can give some ideas about the scope of the topics: Christian buildings have very many different uses; they are found throughout the world, and they take many different forms.

The book can be used alongside the accompanying poster set and alongside books such as:

Christianity: A Pictorial Guide (CEM)
Exploring Churches – Paul and Tessa Clowney (Lion)
Christianity: A World Faith (Lion)
Westhill Project: *Christians*
(Pupils books – 3 (11–14), 4 (14–16), available from Stanley Thornes and Hulton (Freepost) (GR 782), Cheltenham GL53 1BR (Telephone: (0242) 584429)

Age-range – secondary, particularly directed at GCSE students. Adaptability is one intention. Material can be selected and photo-copied, if necessary, to fit in with the appropriate study programme.

The illustrations and posters are intended to provide as comprehensive a glossary as possible of: ground plans, furnishings and fitments, design. The text describes buildings and ways in which they are being used.

Books in this series aim to describe the writers' experiences and responses as well as to inform. We hope that students will touch, smell and wonder at the buildings they visit as well as think about them.

Editor

Four useful addresses for **Teachers**.
For information about World Wide Christianity contact:

Dr. Andrew Walls
The Centre for the Study of Christianity in the Non-Western World
New College
The University
Edinburgh

The Centre for Black and White Christian Partnership
Selly Oak Colleges
Birmingham B29 6LL

Christianity in Britain
A Multi Racial Faith
George Skinner
Centre for Ethnic Studies in Education
Manchester University
Oxford Road
Manchester M13 9PL

Write to this address for an imaginative and useful set of cards:
    "Exploring a Church and Churchyard"
    by Dorothy Jamal – £1.85 inc. p.+p. from
    Dorothy Jamal
    Board of Education
    Church House
    Great Smith Street
    London SW1P 3NZ

GUIDELINES
FOR
STUDENTS

STUDYING CHRISTIAN BUILDINGS IN YOUR AREA: Some Guidelines

1. Draw a sketch map of your area (town, village, district, part of a city etc.) and indicate the major places of worship (all religions).

2. Repeat the sketch map and indicate the different sorts of Christian churches in the area. Shade in where most of the people live.

3. Perhaps you could arrange to meet some of the people who go to these Christian churches and talk to them about why they go and whether or not the building is in a convenient place for them, how often they go and so on.

4. Arrange to explore some of the church buildings. You could probably use the charts on the following pages in order to investigate some of the following features:

   the buildings themselves
   the furnishing and fitments in the buildings
   the uses made of the buildings
   the people connected with the buildings

   With some imagination, this work could lead to producing collages, photographs, diagrams, illustrations, tape recordings. Perhaps you could set up an exhibition for people in your neighbourhood to look at.

   Remember that there are different sorts of Christian buildings.

   The buildings themselves can be very different. There are differences in the ground plan, design and the building style. Some buildings are in a *traditional style*. Others are *modern*. Most church buildings, including the great medieval churches and cathedrals, are *functional*, that is, design is determined by use as well as by technical knowledge.

   The fittings and furnishings inside the buildings can be very different. *Furnishings are determined by the needs of the people* who use any particular building and by the use they make of it. Christianity is a rich and complex religion and different Christian groups approach worship rather differently. Buildings may be quite different in their appearance inside as well as outside.

   Different Christian groups respond differently to the world around them. Some express their attitudes by opening up their buildings to the local community for what might appear to be purely *secular activities*. Others are more inward looking and for whatever the reason, feel it is necessary to keep their buildings for their own use or for explicitly *religious activities*.

5. When you have finished this work you might like to consider questions such as these:

   (i) Do you think that the Christian community really needs buildings?
   Could it manage without them?
   How could it manage without them?
   Why should it try to manage without them if it should?

   (ii) If you were designing a new church what would you want it to look like and how would you like to see the interior furnished?

   (iii) Do you prefer modern church buildings to the older church buildings?

   (iv) What sort of art do you like to see in Christian churches?

   (v) Do you think that most people go to the church nearest to them or do considerations of what the church building is like play a part in their choice of church?

Brenda Lealman

DIFFERENT SORTS OF CHRISTIANS

There are many different sorts of Christians. Each group emphasizes different aspects of Christian experience and belief. These experiences and beliefs are reflected in the buildings they use.

Western Europe
Baptist
Salvation Army
Society of Friends
United Reformed
Church of Scotland
Episcopalian
Church of England
Roman Catholic
Church in Wales
Methodist
Lutheran
Reformed Church of France

India
Mar Thoma
Church of South India

Africa
Aladura
Zimbanguist
Church of Christ in Africa

Eastern Europe and Asia
Armenian
Coptic Orthodox
Maronite
Melkite
Syrian Orthodox
Assyrians

USA
Episcopalian
Roman Catholic
United Church of Christ
Disciples of Christ
Methodist
Southern Baptists
"The Electronic Church"
Mennonite

Just a few of all the Christian groups there are!

CHRISTIAN BUILDINGS IN YOUR AREA: The Buildings

Features:	Roman Catholic	Eastern Orthodox	Church of England	Ecumenical	Methodist	United Reformed	etc.
Position							
Date							
Building materials							
Shape							
How can you tell it is a church?							
Graveyard							
Tower/spire							
Roof							
Windows: shapes/glass							
Bell tower							
Ceiling							
Insides walls: e.g. painted							
What does the building make you feel?							
How much a year is spent on upkeep?							
What is the building called? e.g. mission, chapel, church, Gospel hall							
etc.							

CHRISTIAN BUILDINGS IN YOUR AREA:
The Furnishing and Fitments

Features:	Roman Catholic	Eastern Orthodox	Church of England	Ecumenical	Methodist	United Reformed	etc.
Notice board							
Hymn board							
Font							
Baptism tank							
Seating							
Shape of inside							
Pulpit							
Lectern/ reading desk							
Space for choir							
Musical instruments							
Altar/table							
Candles							
Crosses: What sort?							
Sculptures/paintings							
Memorials							
Flowers							
etc.							

CHRISTIAN BUILDINGS IN YOUR AREA:
Uses made of the Buildings

Uses:	Roman Catholic	Eastern Orthodox	Church of England	Ecumenical	Methodist	United Reformed	etc.
WORSHIP							
Holy Communion/ Eucharist/Mass/ Divine Liturgy/ Lord's Supper/ Family Meal							
Morning service							
Evening service							
Children's arrangements							
Other Services							
Festivals							
Baptisms							
Marriages							
Funerals							
Ordinations							
Others							
SECULAR USES							
etc.							

CHRISTIAN BUILDINGS IN YOUR AREA:
People connected with them

People:	Roman Catholic	Eastern Orthodox	Church of England	Ecumenical	Methodist	United Reformed	etc.
Status of church: e.g. cathedral							
Congregation							
Parish priest/vicar rector/prebendary							
Bishop							
Canon/dean/ provost							
Curate							
Minister/elder							
Other leader							
Choir person							
Musicians							
Lay reader/ lay deacon							
Servers/helpers							
Church wardens							
Dancers							
Artists							
etc.							

BRITISH ISLES

ORKNEY.
CHURCH OF SCOTLAND
CATHEDRAL OF
ST MAGNUS

DUBLIN
ROMAN CATHOLIC
CATHEDRAL OF ST. PATRICK

ST. DAVIDS
ANGLICAN CATHEDRAL
IN WALES.

GREEK ORTHODOX CATHEDRAL
OF ST. SOPHIA
LONDON

N

GUIDELINES
FOR TEACHERS:
EXPLORING
CHRISTIAN BUILDINGS
IN A
PARTICULAR LOCALITY

STARTING TO LOOK AT LOCAL CHURCHES

Note for teachers on how to study some local Christian churches

A day spent visiting several places of worship in your neighbourhood can be excellent value. It can draw together many topics from a Christianity syllabus: not only buildings and symbolism, but also worship and aids to prayer, the origins of different denominations, Christian intiation and social responsibility. Textbook material can be related to familiar local features, the visit can be followed up in a variety of coursework assignments and the trip is cost effective in terms of time and travel expenses.

Building for Worship

In the centre of Oxford, and it is similar in many other towns, there are Christian buildings representing many Christian traditions, including a Community church that worships in a cinema. Any town centre would offer a similar range. The aim of our tour was to understand how they functioned as places of worship; to see how the arrangement, decoration and furnishings expressed 'what God is worth' to believers and how the setting helped them to praise, pray and draw nearer to god and each other. We also wanted to find out how worship is related to service in the community.

Making the most of your visit

There is no substitute for learning by experience and taking part in a service; an empty church building cannot convey the full meaning of worship, or the 'church' as a body of people. However, the building itself may evoke an atmosphere of reverence, mystery or calm; it is interesting to ask why, and given space in the visit to sit quietly, the group may be sensitive to this. Here are a few suggestions for making the most of a midweek visit.

1. Careful preparation and personal contact with the minister or church secretary beforehand has many benefits. Make the purpose of your visit clear; you do not want a talk on medieval church architecture! I found every minister was keen to meet the particular needs of our school group and welcomed us warmly. If the teacher can talk to the clergy or tour leader, visit the church, decide what to see, the length and content of the talk, it is easier to prepare worksheets, and the visit will be productive and satisfying. Taking part in worship and meeting church members beforehand also helped me prepare the groups in the classroom and build up good relations with our hosts.

2. Ideally your guide should be a church member who can relate to young people, involve them in finding out about the building, and stimulate their questions. Encourage the guide to talk about the style of worship in their church, why they have chosen this denomination, what Christian commitment involves for them . . . as well as giving information about the building itself.

3. Showing artefacts can bring a talk about worship alive. One priest put on his eucharistic vestments; a minister laid the Lord's Table for Holy Communion; we saw the crown used at an Orthodox wedding and smelt the incense that lingered after a service.

4. An advantage of a midweek visit is that you are likely to find church members involved in community service, perhaps preparing lunch for pensioners or running a charity shop. We took a morning break in a church coffee shop and had lunch in the garden of the Friends Meeting House.

5. We chose places of worship to visit representing a cross-section of Christian traditions from the Orthodox Church to the Society of Friends. This helped students to grasp the distinctive beliefs of different denominations, and appreciate the variety of ways believers can worship and experience God.

6. After our visit small groups were invited to take part in mid-week services – a Holy Communion in the parish church and a Friends' meeting. This sort of visit might be possible in the Week of Prayer for Christian Unity, or Christian Aid Week, when churches are open midday and ready for visitors.

Some preliminaries for students

1. The group should have a basic knowledge of the architectural features and furniture of a typical parish church and of a non-conformist church, so useful comparisons can be made with 'real' examples and quite different buildings.

2. It is helpful if students understand why there are different denominations today.
They should then be alert to the distinctive features of the building that express the particular beliefs or concerns of that church.

3. If the group has already discussed worship in general, the students will be more sensitive to the symbolism of the building. Many young people will be unfamiliar with religious buildings, and perhaps feel awkward or resistant; preparation can put them at ease and help them to be receptive.

Brenda Hoddinott

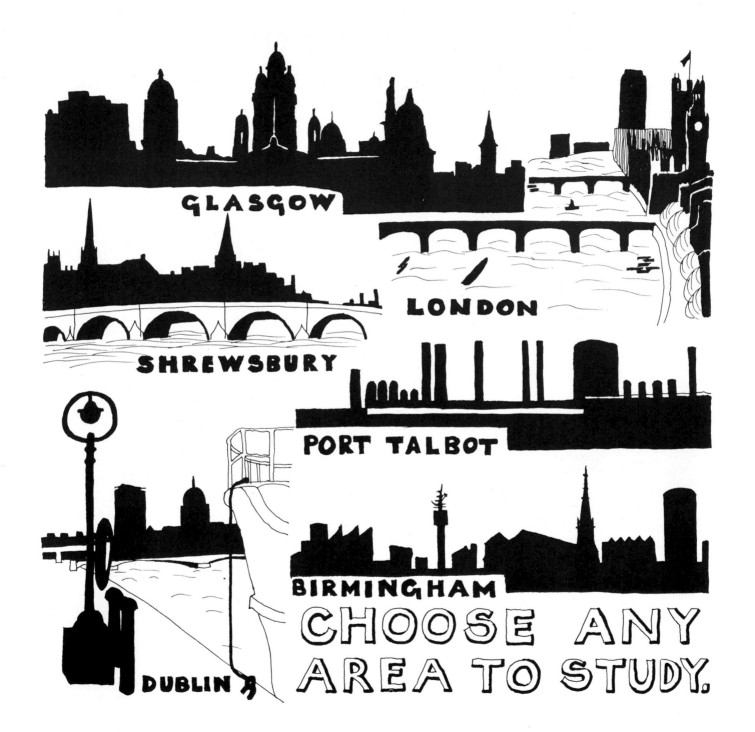

GLASGOW

LONDON

SHREWSBURY

PORT TALBOT

BIRMINGHAM

DUBLIN

CHOOSE ANY AREA TO STUDY.

EXPLORING SOME OF THE CHURCHES OF OXFORD

by Brenda Hoddinott

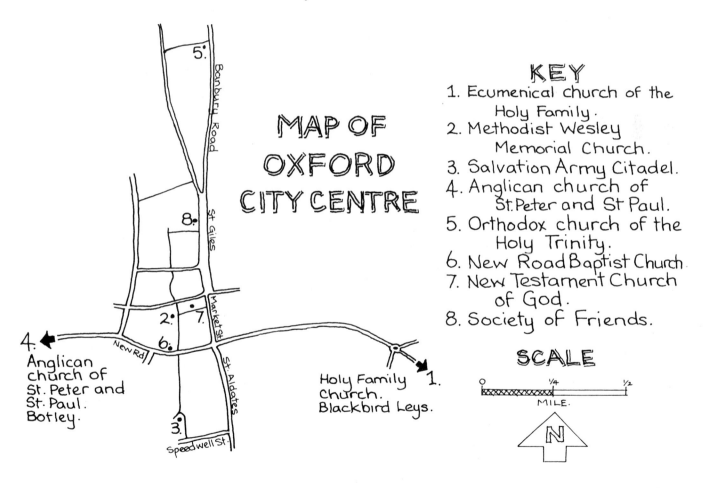

MAP OF OXFORD CITY CENTRE

KEY

1. Ecumenical church of the Holy Family.
2. Methodist Wesley Memorial Church.
3. Salvation Army Citadel.
4. Anglican church of St. Peter and St Paul.
5. Orthodox church of the Holy Trinity.
6. New Road Baptist Church.
7. New Testament Church of God.
8. Society of Friends.

SCALE

0   ¼   ½
MILE.

N

4. Anglican church of St. Peter and St. Paul. Botley.

Holy Family Church. Blackbird Leys.

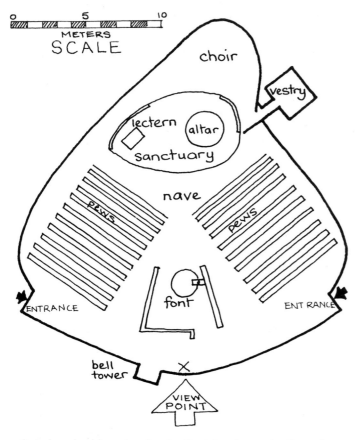

font – large bowl for water where baptism takes place – a baptism makes a
person a member of the Christian church.
pews – seats.
nave – central part of church.
sanctuary – part of church around main altar.
lectern – reading desk.
altar – communion table.
choir – part of church used by singers/organ.
vestry – room where church garments etc. are kept and where clergy/
choir get ready for the services.

THE HOLY FAMILY CHURCH
A LOCAL ECUMENICAL PROJECT

A Community Church
The low church building merges into the surrounding
housing estate of Blackbird Leys, with little to distinguish
it, for the Holy Family Church is about holding together
personal faith and social commitment; it is about the mutual
involvement of church and local community.

The Holy Family is also about Christian community; the
project unites the Anglican, Baptist, Methodists, and URC
churches on the housing estate. Anyone confirmed here
belongs to four denominations.

Sharing Christian Traditions
In this building your attention moves between the altar-
table, the lectern and the font. The room is circular,
designed as a shelter for the church, gathered around the
altar-table. This altar-table was placed on the site before the
building was erected, to show the priority of worship. The
altar-table is so called because the Communion is both
Anglican and a Free Church Service.

The lectern stands alongside the altar to show the balance of
Word and Sacrament in worship.

The font, with the Easter candle, stands in an area shaped
like a coffin – a startling symbol of life out of death. The
font is set amongst the people and is the focus of the most
popular service at Holy Family, the Celebration of New
Life, when families bring babies for baptism or blessing.
This is the largest regular public meeting on the estate; with
typically, 300 or more gathered to worship. The colourful
banners were made by the congregation; the peace banner is
used for vigils at the local US military air base.

A Neighbourhood Centre

During the week the church premises are the busiest advice centre in Oxford. The Good Neighbour Scheme operates from here with a Welfare Rights worker, a drop-in centre for coffee and a chat, a lunch club and neighbourly help service. There is also a community art class, and an adventure playground. All are based here, with church members and other volunteers equally involved. Many people living on the estate are deprived in some way, and the Church is committed to responding to these people's needs.

Worship as a Community Event

Sunday morning communion is an extension of the weekday life of the church. Worship, like the building is a melting-pot of different traditions. Within a pattern of praise and confession, readings and preaching, intercession and communion, there is great variety. An acclamation of praise may replace a hymn or dance-drama express a Bible message. There is dialogue between community and church; local issues are debated, the Welfare Rights worker may speak and the sermon become a debate. God's concern for justice, peace and love is a prominent theme of the songs and prayers.

For me, the high point of the worship was the 'Shalom Circle' At the Peace, we all left our seats and stood in a large circle around the altar; hands joined; we sang 'Shalom, my friends' to each other. The Holy Family church is about creating a community of God's peace in an area of social and personal stress.

Inside the Holy Family Ecumenical Church, Oxford.
Note the shape on the ground plan on the facing page.

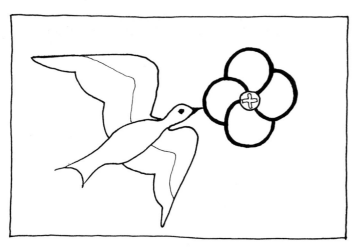

Wall hanging in Holy Family Church, Oxford.
The dove is a symbol of peace.

Follow up work on the Holy Family Church

1. Design a church building for a new housing development.This is an ecumenical project, with finance for a Community Worker.

2. Should a church building be distinctive? Sketch how you think a church should look to passersby. Examine the posters accompanying this booklet.

3. Do you consider that the community-based midweek activities at the Holy Family Church are more important for Christian witness than services on Sunday?

4. Either (a) find out about the Church Urban Fund or (b) Find out how churches in your area are tackling social problems.

5. Members of the local Christian CND group have been arrested for holding vigils to pray for peace inside a US military air base.

Is it right to break the law in a peaceful protest?

If Jesus refused to use force to resist his enemies, should all Christians be nuclear pacifists?

6. Many parents whose babies are baptised at this church rarely come to church again.

Would the minister be right to refuse to baptise children if their parents were not committed Christians? Why do you think these parents want their baby baptised?

NEW ROAD BAPTIST CHURCH

This building, recently refurbished, is a classic expression of Baptist beliefs.

Pulpit
The large pulpit, centrally placed beneath the cross, shows that preaching Christ crucified and risen, proclaiming God's Word and calling people to personal commitment are significant in Baptish worship.

Bible
The Bible lies open on the lectern, for Baptists believe that above all it is through Scripture that God's will is understood. The Communion table is also prominent, as in recent years the Lord's Supper has become fully incorporated into Baptish worship.

Table
At the time of my visit, the people gather around the table, for this Communion meal is a time of giving and sharing with each other. Behind the table are seats for the ministers and lay deacons (elected by the church meeting, they work, with the pastor in a 'team ministry'). The deacons serve the people, who remain seated, with bread and wine; each receives a piece of bread from the same loaf and a small glass of wine, which they eat and drink at the same moment.

Tank
There is a baptismal tank, where those who professed their faith in Christ are received into the Church by immersion.

Cross
A huge cross dominates the Oxford Baptist Church; made in consultation with the church members, it expresses the belief that the church is a gathered community of believers. The crown of thorns, left on the cross affirms faith in the victory of Christ through suffering. The arms of the cross, pick out the different woods used in the church furniture, and express the diversity but unity of Christians in Christ.

Follow up work on the Baptist Church

1. The theme of Freedom runs through Baptist history and church life.

    i. The early Baptists claimed religious liberty and said the Church should be free of state control.

    Where is freedom of conscience still denied? Are there some religious sects that should not be tolerated?

    What should our attitude be to believer who are intolerant of others?

    ii The early Baptists were called dangerous revolutionaries.

    Consider the role that Christians in Eastern Europe have played in the recent mass movements for political liberation.

    Would the Anglican church be a more powerful force for change if its links to the state were cut?

    iii. In the late seventeenth century Baptists in Oxford were fined, imprisoned and their Meeting House wrecked by mobs supporting the king.

    Is any belief worth dying for?

    iv. Find out more about these well known Baptists who have campaigned and suffered for freedom.

        a) John Bunyan, who wrote Pilgrim's Progress while in jail.

        b) Martin Luther King, who was assassinated for his vision that 'all God's children' should be free.

        c) Aida Skroipnikova, the young Reform Baptish in Russia and poet.

2. Look at the cross by Heather Harms on the back cover: this hangs in New Road Baptist Church.
Do you think it is a more powerful symbol of the brutality of the Crucifixion, or the victory of the Resurrection?

THE METHODIST CHURCH

In the illustration, the wall tapestry reads:

I AM NO LONGER MY OWN BUT THINE. AND NOW, O

PUT ME TO WHAT THOU WILT, RANK ME WITH WHOM THOU WILT; PUT ME TO DOING; PUT ME TO SUFFERING; LET ME BE EMPLOYED FOR THEE; OR LAID ASIDE FOR THEE, EXALTED FOR THEE OR BROUGHT LOW FOR THEE; LET ME BE FULL. LET ME BE EMPTY.

LET ME HAVE ALL THINGS; LET ME HAVE NOTHING. I FREELY AND HEARTILY YIELD ALL THINGS TO THY PLEASURE AND DISPOSAL.

GLORIOUS AND BLESSED GOD, FATHER, SON AND HOLY SPIRIT THOU ART MINE AND I AM THINE. SO BE IT. AND THE COVENANT WHICH I HAVE MADE ON EARTH LET IT BE RATIFIED IN HEAVEN. AMEN

Corner in Wesley Memorial Church, Oxford.
The prayer on the wall tapestry is
taken from the Covenant Service.

It was in Oxford that John Wesley and his friends were nicknamed Methodists because of the methodical way in which they prayed, read the Bible, attended to social needs, and he preached at the Methodists' simple Meeting House, close by the present Wesley Memorial Church.

This large Victorian building, with balcony and stained glass, was built when Methodism was flourishing and it reflects the original strengths of the Methodist movement.

The pulpit may have been moved from its high, central position, to one side of the chancel, but preaching and teaching remain essential in Methodist worship. The local lay preachers give the sermon when the itinerant minister is preaching in other churches in the circuit.

The large choir sits in the chancel facing the congregation. Hymn singing is still important for Methodists. Sunday worship is in the Free Church tradition with hymns, Bible readings, sermon and prayers. The choirs can be moved to create space for excellent Christian musicals.

Today the Communion Table is the focus of the building; it is placed in the chancel or on a dais in the centre of the congregation. Communion is held twice a month.

The font is used for infant baptism which Methodists recognise as a sacrament. Adults are received into full Church membership by the minister with the option of the laying on of hands. Members join a class meeting or regular weekday fellowship group, another strength of Methodism.

Each year at the Convenant Service, Methodists renew their allegance to God. A colourful tapestry with the words of the Covenant prayer of dedication hangs in the church. This prayer of John Wesley begins "I am no longer mine, but thine . . ."

Membership tickets remind Methodists of their responsibility to serve Christ in the community. This church is a base for many caring organisations and through its own clubs, the church supports physically handicapped and elderly people and young families.

Follow up work on the Methodist Church

1. John Wesley said 'The world is my parish'.
Find out about his life as a travelling preacher and his
message that God's love was for everyone.

2. Other churches have come to recognise the value of
small midweek house meetings for prayer and Bible study.

How can such groups support church members?

Would non-church goers feel 'at home' in such a group?

The first Christians met to worship in each others' homes.

Would you find it more or less easy to worship in a house
group?

3. The Bible is central to all Methodist beliefs.

Some people believe that every word is inspired, others that
we must get behind outdated words to discover how the
Bible applies today.

What value do you think the Bible has today?

WESLEY
MEMORIAL
CHURCH .OXFORD.

SALVATION ARMY

Outreach
The Salvation Army was formed to bring the good News of the Love of God to the poor of London's East End and I found the headquarters or Citadel of the Oxford Corps in a city centre area where the homeless gather. The centre was busy; a pensioners lunch club, a charity shop, coffee lounge, youth club are run by enthusiastic volunteers who share responsibility for the Corps activities with the full-time commanding officers (both ladies).

But the heart of the Citadel is the Worship Hall, for personal Christian commitment motivates the Army's Social work and Sunday worship empowers their outreach.

I attended the enrolment of a Salvation Army soldier during the Sunday morning service, or Holiness Meeting. This reflected Salvationists' emphasis on living a disciplined Christian life, but the meeting was not dull or exclusive. Visitors were warmly welcomed and worships was joyful lively and informal.

The Worship Hall
The worship hall was simply furnished; rows of chairs faced a platform where the commanding officers and local officers sat. Major Dixon led the worship and preached from the reading desk. The Songster Brigade (choir) and the band also sat on the platform. The walls were bare, except for the Salvation Army Crest and the flags of the corps. Their motto 'Blood and Fire' boldly declared Salvationists' distinctive beliefs.

There was no altar; instead a large bible lay open on the Holiness Table, in front of the platform – a sign that Salvationists draw near to God through hearing his message read and preached from the bible, rather than through a sacramental meal.

Joy
'Sing so as to make the whole world hear,' said William Booth, and Salvationists still make particular use of music in worship. We praised God enthusiastically, with simple words set to favourite tunes and accompanied by a brass band or organ; other songs were quiet and devotional. The Songsters contributed Gospel music, focusing on personal commitment to Christ and witness, all beautifully and sincerely offered to inspire, cheer or comfort with a simple message. Young people were actively involved playing in the band and singing with the music group.

Repentance and Commitment
The mercy seat is unique to a Citadel. It is a plain wooden bench behind the Holiness Table. People are invited to pray here for forgiveness for repentance is seen as the key to new life, make a commitment to follow Christ. At this service 12 Junior Soldiers, young teenagers, knelt with the Brigade Officer to renew their enrolment promises. It took courage to make such a public commitment, but these young people had the encouragement of the Corps.

An Enrolment
After free prayer led by the officers, a Bible reading and powerfully delivered address from a visiting Officer from the Carribean, came the Enrolment. This is a ceremony to strengthen Christian commitment and admit to full membership of the Army. The candidate a spritely pensioner stood at the reading desk, the Colour Sergeant behind, as Major Dixon read the Articles of War. Hand raised shoulder high, the new soldier solemnly promises to keep them Articles and signed them. Then Elsie gave her testimony, choosing a short poem to express her personal experience of God's love; witness is another important feature of worship for Salvationists.

Sunday worship does not only happen 'in church' for these Christians. They hold two open air meetings wherever they can reach people with the Gospel and visit hospitals, prisons, public houses with their music and witness.

Follow up work on the Salvation Army
(The Salvation Army's own educational material is good for pupil research.)

1. Can you find out what the Motto means, the significance of signs on the Crest and why the flag is blue, red and yellow?

2. The preacher was West Indian – in how many countries will you find the Salvation Army?

3. What are the promises made in the Articles of War? Discuss the usefulness today of the strict code of behaviour Soldiers must keep.

4. Some Christians wear a lapel badge, the Salvationists a

uniform. How do you think this affects their own lives and other peoples' attitudes to them? Should Christians make their beliefs public?

5. Would you call their Worship Hall a Church?
Is their anything essentially Christian missing from their worship?

6. Major Dixon talked a lot about personal commitment and involvement. What will that mean for members of the Corps in terms of time, lifestyle beliefs . . .

7. The Salvation Army is well known for its social work. find out about it's activities in your area.

8. Join the crowd at an open air meeting. Report back on your impressions – try to talk to a Salvationst at the meeting.

The Salvation Army.
The Worship Hall at the Oxford Citadel.
A large Bible lies open and table below the lectern-pulpit.
Behind the table is the mercy seat.

A Lay Reader, preaching during Family Communion at Church of SS Peter and Paul, Oxford.

The Procession and Reading of the Gospel during Family Communion at Church of SS Peter and Paul, Oxford.

FAMILY EUCHARIST IN AN ANGLICAN CHURCH, SS PETER AND PAUL

Buildings and Change

As new forms of worship have been introduced in the Anglican Church in recent years, so there have been changes in the design and arrangement of many parish churches. Perhaps the altar has been moved forward, or a nave altar introduced for the Eucharist; rows of fixed pews replaced by free standing chairs grouped around the altar; space provided for drama, dance or a music group. These alterations reflect a new understanding of the Church as a family, sharing in corporate worship at the Eucharist, as well as a renewal of religious experience expressed in spontaneous, informal prayer and praise. Yet Anglican worship is characterised by balance; using a service book gives worship a formal structure and roots in tradition. Candles, processions, vestments and robed choirs lend dignity and reverence, and there are pauses for quiet, private reflection.

Word and Sacrament

The traditional division of an Anglican church into two areas, nave and chancel, expresses the shape of the Eucharist: the first part, the Ministry of the Word; the second part, the Ministry of the Sacrament. The clergy and choir lead the service from the chancel. On a low platform in the sanctuary beyond the communion rail, stands the altar, or Communion Table, the focus of worship and the building. The church I attend has a stone altar, symbolising the death of Jesus; but above hangs a cross from where Christ reigns as king, a sign of his victory over death.

God's Work and our words

The lectern and pulpit are positioned prominently in the nave for the congregation to give attention to the Bible readings, and the address.

Family Eucharist on a Sunday morning begins with the people speaking to God in hymns, and prayers. After listening to God's message for them in the redings and sermon, they respond by declaring their faith in the Creed.

Prayers of intercession are led by a member of the congregation and there is scope for songs, drama and dance to proclaim God's word for today.

The Family Meal

Attention then moves to the altar, and the Communion meal. To prepare for this, everyone exchanges the Peace or greeting, a sign that the church is Christ's body, united by love; the offertory follows a reminder that worship means giving our lives to God.

The pace changes; an atmosphere of reverence and mystery builds up as the priest says the Prayer of Thanksgiving and consecrates the bread and wine.

Kneeling at the communion rail to receive the sacrament, some may recall the past and how Christ's death and resurrection changed history. Others may focus on the presence of Christ at his table, ready to meet us, and satisfy our need for refreshment. Others find that grouped together, sharing the same food, strengthens the bonds of the church family.

Follow up work on the Anglican Church

There is such variety amongst Anglican churches it is difficult to generalise.

1. Compare the furniture, arrangement and decoration in several churches. what features indicate different beliefs about the Sacrament?

2. Is there evidence of informal styles of worship? Has the building been altered in the last few years, and why? How would you alter it for worship?

THE ORTHODOX CHURCH

Worship through Symbols

If worship is about standing in awe before the holiness of God, then an Orthodox church offers a setting in which it is natural to praise, adore and honour God in his transcendent majesty.

The use of symbols to penetrate this world and allow the believer to join in 'the worship of heaven' is at the heart of Orthodox worship. Ceiling and walls covered with sparkling mosaics and colourful frescoes, all dominated by the majestic figure of Christ, Pantocrator, express the sovereignty of God. Flickering candles, glowing other wordly icons, incense and antiphonal chant, evoke the mystery of God.

Even at a quiet Vigil, in the relatively simple Orthodox church in Oxford, I could appreciate the goal of worship – to focus on God Himself and make his eternal reality present.

Easter is Today

Building and liturgy combine to praise Christ risen and with his people for evermore. The Oxford church is octagonal because Christ rose on the eighth day and God's

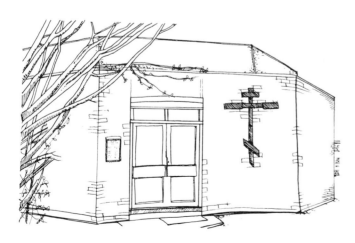

The Orthodx Church of the Holy Trinity and Annunciation, Oxford.

New Creation began. When I visited, the church was full of light from candles, lamps and a large candelabra, another sign of resurrection life. The Easter story was read and praise was repeatedly offered to Christ, the Light of the World and the conqueror of death. Every Sunday is a celebration of the resurrection life.

Access to God

It may seem that the congregation is excluded from worship by the icon screen or iconastasis between the nave and the sanctuary. the nave where we stood, represents the created world; the sanctuary beyond the screen, represents the kingdom of God, the eternal reality. However, the priest explained that although this screen marked a distinction, it is not a barrier.

The Image of God in us all

But everyone, not only the saints, is made in the image of God. That likeness can be restored if human beings reflect the life of the saints; but absolute respect is due not only to the saints but to each individual. This was vividly expressed in the liturgy, when the priest moved around the church, sensing not only each icon, but each person in the congregation.

Pierced by three doors and painted with icons, the iconastasis tells the story of salvation. On the central Royal Door is an icon of the Annunciation, to show how God entered the world, to reunite God and humans in his incarnate Son.

During the liturgy there was much movement, backwards and forwards through the doors, symbolising our access to God. The priest carried the book of the gospels into the nave for the readings. A Divine Liturgy brings the sacrament from the sanctuary for the people to receive.

Transparent Symbols

The icons all around the church and covering the screen are important for making God's presence more real. These pictures of Jesus, Mary and the saints look unnatural – They are designed to express a Saint's inner life, not to be a portrait. Central on every iconastasis you will see Christ, represented as a child with his Mother, and, holding the book of the Gospels, as teacher, judge and ruler of all. He is the true image or icon of God.

Everyone took a candle as they entered, walked to an icon stand, crossed themselves, bowed and kissed the icon, leaving a lighted candle beside it. Honour given to the apostle or saint passes through the 'likeness' or icon, to unite the worshipper with the reality, God.

Icon

Follow up work on the Orthodox Church

1. The Orthodox Church in Oxford does not hold special services for children. They feel that symbols allow children and adults to respond to God at their own level.

Also children and their parents are free to move around, come and go.

What do you think would hold a child's attention?

Do you find a picture or candle a better aid to prayer and worship than readings and talks?

2. Worship seems to go on apart from the congregation, as the choir chants the prayers, psalms and hymns and the people hardly join in.
Do you need to <u>doing</u> something to be involved in worship?

How can the congregation contribute to the worship without outwardly appearing to join in?

3. The Liturgy uses very traditional language.

The prayers were general and did not refer to specific problems or needs today. The traditional faith was reaffirmed in the words of the Creeds.

Do you agree that worship should be modern? What do you mean by 'modern'?

Are there any parts you would not change in the Orthodox Liturgy?

4. Read the account of Isaiah's call to be a prophet in the Temple (Isaiah 6).

How did he catch a glimpse of God's holiness through worship?

Discuss experiences of awe, wonder and worship.

How can a building evoke or express praise, awe, wonder?

PENTECOSTAL PRAISE: THE NEW TESTAMENT CHURCH OF GOD

Church Growth
The New Testament Church of God (the largest Pentecostal denomination in the UK) has outgrown its building in Oxford and hires a hall for worship. Pentecostal churches, are now the fastest growing Christian bodies worldwide. When I visited, I could see that the hall was easily adapted for worship. The pastor sat on the stage and led worship from a reading desk. The only symbol was a cross on the lectern. The preacher, a layman, in a lounge suit, sat beside him. There was a row of cushions in front of the stage, where people might kneel for the 'laying on of hands' to receive the gift of the Holy Spirit or of healing. The choir sat to one side, wearing white hats and black suits. The congregation was smartly dressed, giving a sense of occasion. Music was provided by keyboard, guitar and tambourine, but the congregation knew the songs and needed no leading.

The Choir singing Gospel music at the New Testament Church of God, Oxford.

Enjoying God
Worship was foremost an occasion to praise God, in singing, prayer and acclamation. We began, continued and ended with lively choruses and hymns; we clapped, swayed and raised hands in praise. 'Do you feel better?' the Pastor asked; the enthusiasm for God was unaffected and infectious.

Vitality in the Spirit
The Pentecostalist movement is distinctive for its belief in 'baptism in the Holy Spirit', an individual experience of God's power filling, renewing and empowering the believer. This is accompanied by outward signs of the Spirit's presence such as the early church experienced. People chose songs, offered extempore prayers with rising emotion, occasionally praised God in tongues, and one lady gave a prophecy (a message directly from God, urging us to deeper commitment). The preacher described physical healings he had received in worship. Everyone was eager to share their personal faith and love for Jesus and acclamations of 'Praise you Lord', or 'Thank you Jesus' punctuated the prayers and the sermon.

Powerful Preaching
Particular attention was given to the Bible reading; we stood and formally sang the Gloria. The sermon was Bible-based and on a triumphant theme: we should seek the power of the Spirit to overcome 'mountains of difficulty'. the preacher relied on personal experience, not scholarship to expound his text. We looked up references and the congregation could recite passages by heart.

It was not surprising to find close friendship amongst a small West Indian community, when we walked around to share fellowship; I was warmly greeted by many there. When we sang the chorus

'For I'm building a people of power'

it seemed particularly appropriate to this church.

Follow up work on the Pentecostal Church

1. The growth of the Pentecostal Church has been described as an explosion, especially in the developing world. Pentecostalists make up the largest group of Protestants, world wide. Can you account for their success?

2. Speaking in tongues, miracles of healing, visions and prophecy are regarded as signs of being filled with the Holy Spirit. How much credibility and value do you give such experiences? How might they make a believer a 'better Christian'?

3. Pentecostal worship expresses certainty of God's victory and promises Christians blessings here and hereafter. How can this be reconciled with the reality of evil and suffering around us?

4. Find out about Pentecostalist social outreach at the Teen Challenge Centre, New York, (see the book, *The Cross and the Switchblade* by D. Wilkerson).

5. Is Christian healing an alternative to medicine? What part might prayer and faith play in healing? for Pentecostalists, healing is also a release from personal powers of evil. Does sin cause illness?

6. The Charismatic Movement with its rediscovery of the gifts of the Holy Spirit, is having a great influence on the traditional churches. What is the appeal of, for example, personal religious experience, free worship, signs and wonders, emphasis on biblical authority?

7. Why do young Christians flock to the Green Belt Musical festival?

THE RELIGIOUS SOCIETY OF FRIENDS

All you need for worship at a Friends' Meeting is a room and some chairs, for worship means sitting quietly together, and in the shared silence listening and waiting for the spirit in each person to lead to a deeper understanding or ourselves and God.

'Something of God'

Your first impression of worship with the Friends might be that they have abandoned religion, for there is no altar, no pulpit, no font, not even a cross. There are no hymns. But the reverse is true; the Friends have abolished the 'ordinary' and treat all life as holy. They believe that there is 'that of God' in everyone – some call it the Light of God or Holy Spirit; God's presence can be continually experienced in all times and places. there is no need for the Eucharist to make Christ's presence real and no need for clergy, for each of us must find our own path to truth, led by the light of God in us. I certainly found that Friends base their whole lives on spiritual values.

A Place to Wait on God

Friends can meet anywhere, but in Oxford they have a purpose-built Meeting House. It is a simple, wood panelled hall, with rows of benches arranged around a table. Midweek worship is held in the Garden Room, a sunny lounge overlooking a quiet garden. On the central table are copies of the Bible, the Book of Christian Discipline (a guide to Friends' beliefs and lifestyle) and other books that might be read in worship. The Bible is essential reading for Friends because they find their simple faith on the life and teaching of Jesus, but its authority is secondary to the guidance of the inner light of God.

A Meeting House is not consecrated, yet when we entered there was a hush. The simplicity of the room created a peaceful atmosphere in which there is freedom and space to find the still centre in ourselves, which for Friends is an experience of God.

Worship in Stillness

Our worship began without formal introduction: Gently we settled our bodies and minds and became quiet and expectant. I found the silence relaxed, not strange. We were journeying inwards together. After twenty minutes, a

Friends gather for prayer at the Meeting House in Oxford.

Friend felt moved by the spirit of the meeting to say a few sentences. Speaking from experience, he encouraged us not to despair in times of disappointment, for as 'instruments of Holy Spirit' there is a wider purpose for our lives. Spoken contributions like this are called 'ministry'. Anyone is free to speak, pray, read from the Bible or another book, if they feel it will help others to achieve a greater awareness of God. Although 'ministry' is spontaneous, Friends often find that a 'minister' speaks directly to their needs; we can communicate deep feelings in silence.

Quietness followed, while we applied the ministry to ourselves. Worship ended as an Elder shook hands with his neighbour and we all greeted each other. It had been renewing to take time apart with others, and see life in its total perspective.

Friends' Concerns

The quietness of the meeting gave way to a friendly charity lunch. Friends are well known for their commitment to social reform. If the spirit of God is in us all, we must respect every life. A deep concern for peace is fundamental to the Friends' lifestyle. This Quaker Meeting has a Peace Centre shop and resources room, and is open house for many organisation all faiths that share their concern for peace, justice, world development and ecology.

Follow up work on the Society of Friends

1. It is said that meditation can help you explore your deepest experience.

Can you, for a brief time, find and return to the still centre of yourself?

Do you find silence strange, distracting, relaxing? How can you gather your thoughts?

2. The Meeting House is not consecrated, yet it has the atmosphere of a holy place. Can you suggest why?

3. An attender I talked to said the Friends meet the needs of people who have a feeling for faith but want to be free to question. Do you agree?

Friends say the church's doctrines about Christ may be unhelpful to people seeking an experience of God.

Do you agree? Are there some teachings we must accept even if we don't understand them, or they have not been our experience?

4. Is it fair to describe this as 'do-it-yourself' faith?

5. Friends say they are returning to the simple life of love for God and others that Jesus taught.

Do you think theirs is the way Jesus intended for his followers?

6. Consider the relevance today of Friends' simple life-style and commitment to peace.

Students relaxing in the garden of the Friends' Meeting House, Oxford, during a visit there.

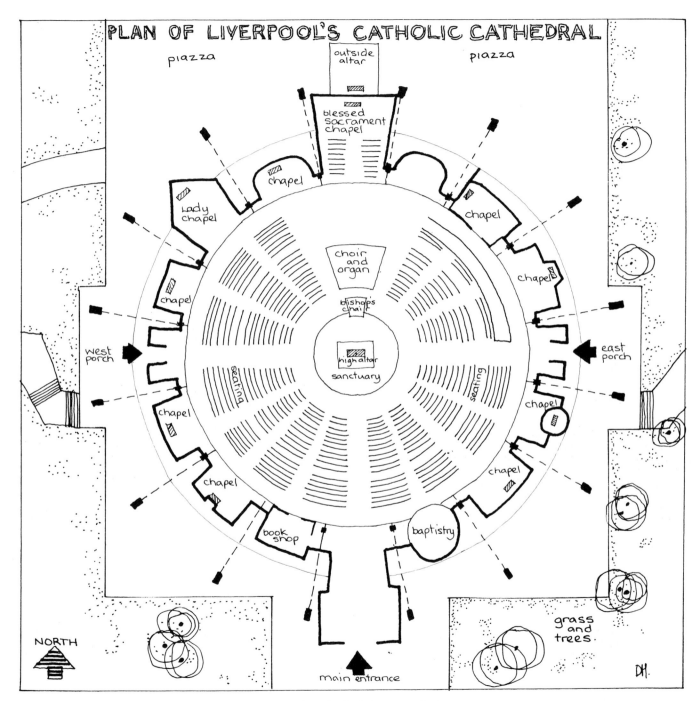

PLAN OF LIVERPOOL'S CATHOLIC CATHEDRAL

piazza

outside altar

piazza

blessed sacrament chapel

chapel

Lady chapel

chapel

choir and organ

chapel

chapel

bishop's chair

chapel

west porch

chapel

high altar

sanctuary

seating

seating

east porch

chapel

chapel

chapel

book shop

baptistry

chapel

NORTH

grass and trees.

main entrance

DH.

Outside view of Cathedral shown on facing page.

EXPLORING
A
CATHEDRAL

PADDY'S WIGWAM: THE METROPOLITAN CATHEDRAL OF CHRIST THE KING, LIVERPOOL
(Roman Catholic)

Note: It is not size or age which makes a cathedral but the presence of a bishop's seat (cathedra) *or centre of authority. It is the main church of an area, administrative and pastoral, and which is called a diocese.* (Editor).

Two strikingly different cathedrals stand at each end of a street called Hope dominating the city skyline of Liverpool. Clergy and congregation of both work together to show their loyalty to and love of God in partnership, worship and service, in liturgy, music, in industrial and economic challenges. One cathedral is Anglican; one is Roman Catholic. We are going to explore the Catholic cathedral, built in 19XX.

In concrete, wood, stone, metal, candlegrease and fabric this striking building known affectionately as 'Paddy's Wigwam', proclaims to those who visit and/or worship in it, what a Christian believes and practices. The discerning eye, prompted by the right questions, sees beneath the physical beauty to the thoughts and feelings of those who know what it means to have a faith to live by.

The Entrance
We find ourselves at the foot of the huge facade of the bell tower. The sliding entrance doors of bronzed fibre glass remind us of the source of our knowledge of Jesus' earthly life, for they bear the winged emblem of the four evangelists – man, lion, ox, eagle. In the stone above is carved a huge cross, flanked by the crosses of the two thieves. Linked by crowns. They proclaim the triumphant ending of the evangelists' story – the resurrection of Christ and the resurrection of humankind. Above, the four bells, named after the four evangelists proclaim the re-telling of their story.

Inside
Passing through the low doors and a small porch, we suddenly find ourselves in the massive, circular interior, unbroken by columns our eyes drawn ever upwards from the central altar to the top of the cupular, from cross and tomb to the glory of Christ, King of Heaven, Proclaimer of Resurrection. The uninterrupted view of the central high altar leaves us in no doubt that Christ's sacrifice and resurrection lie at the heart of the new Catholic liturgy, inspired by the thinking of Vatican II. People and clergy are linked together as they surround it in one great circle. Even the archbishop's chair forms part of the circle. The whole design ensures maximum participation by all. The architecture and furnishings are more than works of art. They are themselves part of the worship.

The Altar
Upon the rectangular block of white marble which forms the altar, the long-stemmed narrow crucifix of Elizabeth Frink does not disturb the uninterrupted view of the worshippers, but its arms are spread wide. The cathedral has a night shelter in the crypt which feeds and houses the homeless. Symbolically, those who worship there, laity and clergy, may bring their own burdens to the altar and also take up the burdens of the world.

Above the altar is a suspended tubular space frame canopy, reminiscent of the crown of thorns and also offering protection to the altar. Soaring above them both is the lantern tower of coloured glass. Its continuous abstract pattern in every imaginable colour proclaims that God is one. There are just three beams of white light that show the oneness of Father, Son and Holy Spirit. By day, the sunlight floods the stone with a kaleidescope of colour. By night, the illuminated tower becomes a beacon, proclaiming warmth, safety, companionship to all.

The Side Chapels
Many of the side chapels were empty or unfinished at the consecration. The generosity and talents of a living community have furnished them. These chapels include:

The Baptising Chapel: stands near the entrance, for it is through baptism that one joins the Family of Believers. The design is simple and strong. The font is of the same marble as the altar. Except at Easter, the Paschal candle stands here. That candle, lit at Easter Sunday to proclaim the light contradicting the darkness of death and despair, also stands beside the coffin at a funeral. The great symbol of hope of resurrection.

The Chapel of St. Patrick: reminds us of the origin of many of the worshipping families. It is one of the three chapels containing confessionals designed as part of the encircling walls which face the altar, the sign that Christ's sacrifice brought reconciliation and forgiveness.

The Chapel of St. Thomas Aquinas: the teacher's chapel. The gift of the school teachers of the diocese, signifying the importance of education and religious education if believers are to be fully active followers of Christ. Beside the Cathedral stands the Education Centre promoting open-sided and exciting Religious Education.

The Chapel of the Blessed Sacrament: is lit by two large triangular windows of abstract designs. The 'Gothic' Anglican cathedral has many narrative elements in its windows acted as teachers to those who could not read. Much of the glass of the Roman Catholic cathedral acknowledges the age of literacy in which Britain lives and uses designs for visitors to interpret and meditate upon in their own way.

The Lady Chapel: is flanked by tall narrow windows whose golden glass reflects the warmth, safety and gentleness of motherhood. The deep reverence of Roman Catholics for Mary is shown at the close of Sunday evening worship when choir and congregation stand before the ceramic statue of Mary and the boy Jesus and sing in her honour.

The Chapel of Joseph: not only reminds us of Jesus' earthly father. Its vertical pine boarding, gray slate altar and quarry tiles remind us of the craftsmen – like Joseph – who built the cathedral, and proclaim the dignity of work.

The Chapel of Pentecost: is surmounted by a magnificent brightly coloured hanging commemorating both the opening of the cathedral on Whit Sunday 1967 and the Pope's visit on Whit Sunday 1982. The Holy Spirit in the form of the Dove of Peace, descends on the people of God – on Pope John Paul II flanked by the Anglican Bishop, David Sheppard as well as Cardinal Hume, Archbishop Warlock, the Organist etc.

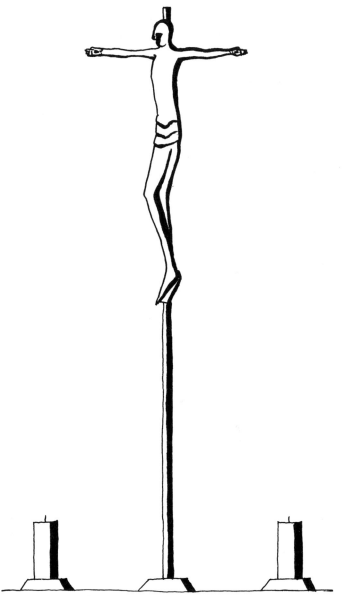

Long-stemmed crucifix on the altar in Liverpool R.C. Cathedral.

On Whit Sunday of the following year – that dove of peace became a wooden anchor of hope, carried along Hope Street from one cathedral to the other. A cross was worked into its design bearing the word Hope and fresh shoots from the foot of the cross – new hope, new life, new beginnings of friendship, reconciliation, fellowship, action.

The Chapel of St. Anne: dedicated to the Virgin's mother is the gift of the children, its tapestry of her made by local school children. The holy water stays was the gift of Pope Paul VI and shows five scenes from Christ's life connected with water – his baptism, the feast at Caia, the well in Sameria, the pool of Bethsaide and the washing of the disciples feet.

The Crypt
The original crypt was incorporated in the new design. We must leave the main cathedral and enter it by another door.

Concerts are held in the West Chapel; the night shelter is there. Its most striking feature is the huge six tons marble disc which covers the entrance to the Chapel of Relics where three former archbishops are buried. We can see the tomb inside, and the disc rolls open, reminding us of the stone rolled away from Christ's tomb when he rose from the dead, as they will rise.

People of the Cathedral
But the real cathedral is the body of visitors, worshippers, those inspired by its symbolic and liturgical message, by the life of Christ told by the four evengelists. Musicians, dancers, actors glorify God and humankind whom he created in his image. Its well stocked shop is often crowded. Its basement café caters for the thousands of visitors specially the school parties who remember it chips if not is symbols.

Vida Barnett

SOME ACTIVITIES WHICH TAKE PLACE IN CHRISTIAN BUILDINGS

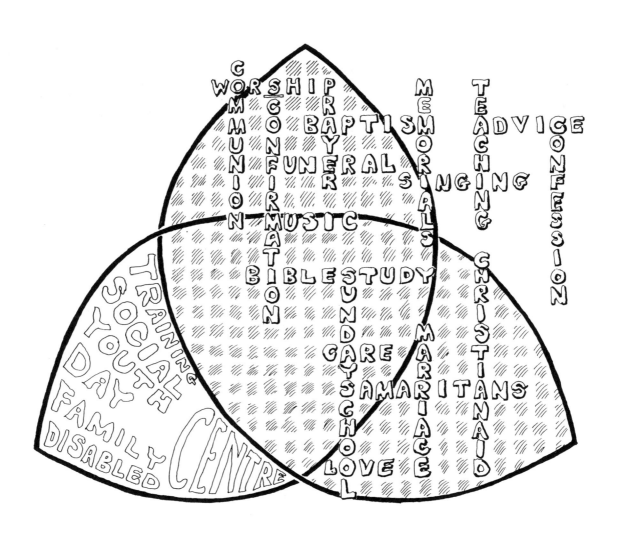

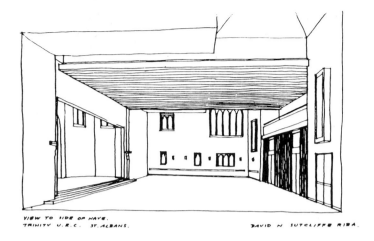

VIEW TO SIDE OF NAVE.
TRINITY U.R.C. ST. ALBANS.

DAVID N SUTCLIFFE RIBA.

TRINITY UNITED REFORMED CHURCH, ST. ALBANS

Trinity is a living and developing community

In the Gospel portraits of Jesus we see certain ideas and qualities: love, acceptance, foregiveness, wholeness, sharing friendship, care, liberation . . . We believe that these both reveal the nature of God and determine the task of the church: to embody the qualities and ideas of Jesus. We are invited to co-operate with God in the transformation of people and societies. That is why Trinity Church is concerned with friendship, caring, justice, ending racial discrimination, housing the homeless, caring for the environment, feeding the hungry, and with being a healing and accepting community.

Trinity at Worship

People coming to worship at 10.00 a.m. on Sunday morning have the choice of either a service in the tradition of Reformed Churches – prayers, hymns, Bible readings, weighty sermon – or of attending Worship in the Round, an experimental form of worship and learning for children and adults.

Both services are on the same theme. At 10.45 a.m. both congregatons unite for pastoral news and a celebration of the theme for the day. The Lord's Supper, to which the whole congregation, including children, is invited, is celebrated on the first Sunday of each month. There is a creche for children under three years; the morning ends with coffee. (Trinity was featured in a television programme about children and Holy Communion.)

Worship in the Round is led mostly by the people of the church – about 45 take part in leardership each year – who plan and prepare together in groups. Questions and discussion are encouraged, as well as the sharing of convictions and experience. A great variety of educational techniques are used. The themes of worship reflect the concerns of the people and of the surrounding society as well as the festivals of the Christian year.

The church has the services as oganist of a professional musician and a wide range of other musicians and people talented in a craft or in art. A number of special services are arranged for instance on Christmas Eve and Maundy

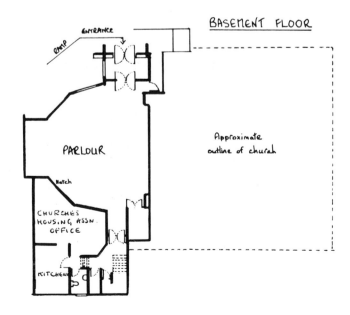

BASEMENT FLOOR

ENTRANCE

RAMP

PARLOUR

Hatch

CHURCHES HOUSING ASSN. OFFICE

KITCHEN

Approximate outline of church

Thursday. Baptisms, marriages and funerals are arranged as requested, though the use of church for the latter two is somewhat restricted because of the regular use of the building.

Celebration has an important place in the family life of the church and is reflected in the Church family days or weekends which are arranged twice a year on major themes and in the annual church outing.

Ministry

The Minister is joined in the pastoral care of the congregation by twelve Elders (men and women). We believe that everyone in the church has a contribution to make – at work, at home, at leisure, in exercising political responsibility – in the work of the church, and that this is part of the work of God in the world.

The life of the church is largely determined by the Church Meeting which meets on ten occasions during the year and is responsible for all the major decisions in the church's life. The meeting of the people of the church emphasises the church's belief that everyone in the church has responsibility for its future and has a ministry to exercise. A Confirmation/Church Membership group is held each autumn. The major emphases in the church's life are decided on a two year cycle with an assessment of progress being made before new decisions are reached.

Meetings for Prayers held at 7.00 a.m. and followed by breakfast on Wednesday mornings during four months of the year have made a remarkable contribution to the church's ministry. Occasional series of Bible Study and house groups are arranged.

Political and social commitment

The major local and national issues of the day are part of the church's agenda. Social care, justice, peace, love of neighbour and sharing which are central themes of the Bible must be expressed in political decision making and action, as well as in personal life. Therefore, without expressing party preference, the church encourages active political discussion and commitment. The housing, community charge and education bills, proposals concerning the NHS, the future of the local hospital, community care and under-age drinking have been discussed in recent Church Meetings. The church has hosted several public protest meetings.

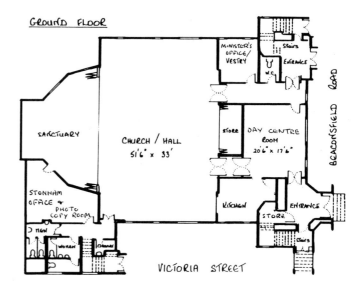

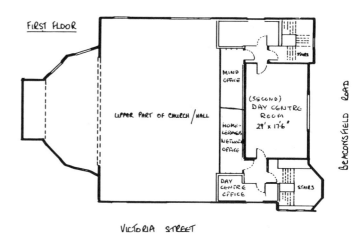

An Accepting Church

WE BELIEVE . . .
in the equal
worth of every
individual as
a child of God.

- The work
  of the church is shared by a
  full-time minister, twelve elected elders
  and every member of the church through
  the Church Meeting.

- Children and young people are
  encouraged to take a full part in the life
  of the church with the adults.

- The church encourages inter-faith
  dialogue and has friendly links with
  people of other faiths.

- Trinity is a member of the St Albans
  Council of Churches and people of many
  different denominational backgrounds
  have found a home with us.

We believe that in taking an active political role in the community we are being faithful both to the Bible and to our own tradition as a nonconformist church.

Day Centre
As an extension of its belief that the church's life should reflect the life of Jesus, the church has established a Day Centrte which is used on different days by mentally ill, mentally handicapped and elderly confused people who are referred by their health visitors or social workers. There are also regular meetings for carers and Bangladeshi mothers and a play group for their children. There are about 110 referred Centre users each week. This Centre is very comfortably furnished and equipped with craft, music, games, nursery and cooking facilities and a laundry.

The Centres are staffed by an Organiser and a Deputy Organiser, both of whom are employed full time, and by about thirty volunteers. The Centre has a separate budget of about £36,000 per year.

Other users of the building
The Trinity Community Play Group meets on four mornings a week.

The St. Albans homelessness network, the St. Albans and District Churches housing association, MIND and the St. Albans Stonham Housing Association use offices in the church.

A variety of interest groups use the premises each week, about 700 people in all. Because of the extensive use made of the church premises the church is committed to follow through a planned cycle of decoration and refurbishment

We enjoy each other's company at our Barn Dances, Harvest Suppers, Carol Singing and Bank Holiday walks.

A Caring Church

Links

Trinity is a member of the St. Albans Council of Churches and a supporters of Christian Aid. The church is a significant provider of leadership in the Council of Churches, Christian Aid, Hostel for the homeless, Homelessness Network, the Good Neighbour Scheme, Girl Guides Movement and World Development Movement.

Members of Trinity have personal links with Christians in other European countries, Africa, Asia and the Americas which enrich the life of the community. The church frequently welcomes overseas visitors and contributes significantly to the provision of accommodation for a Nicaraguan who studies at Hatfield Polytechnic. The Minister has been encouraged to accept invitations to lecture in Nicaragua and India.

Two groups of people from Trinity undertake voluntary service on a regular basis at a hospital for long term mentally ill people.

Trinity contributes about £5,500 a year to work in other places, its major commitment being to world development

The Revd John Sutcliffe

WE BELIEVE . . . that the task of the Church is to reflect the nature of God made known through Jesus Christ.

To this end Trinity runs or provides accommodation for:

- a Day Centre serving the mentally ill, the mentally disabled, the elderly confused, the terminally ill and their carers;

- a Family Centre, providing cooking, laundry and nursery facilities for homeless families;

- a Community Playgroup;

- a Social Club for patients at Shenley Hospital;

- St Albans and District Homelessness Network;

- two Housing Associations;

- a 'MIND' worker.

The whole church contributes to and benefits from a network of individual pastoral care.

LEOMINSTER PRIORY

Leominster Priory is everyone's idea of a typical country parish church. A substantial part of the building dates back to 1130 and the whole church existed in more or less its present form by 1320. It is set in a large churchyard tucked away behind the main street of this busy little Herefordshire town.

But as soon as you step inside the church you realise that this is not just a relic of the past. Displayed on a noticeboard are a set of photographs of all the members of the congregation. This is obviously a community of people. And you only have to glance at the 24-page magazine which covers nine linked parishes to realise that it is an active community. Of course it has the usual 'churchy' things about harvest festivals and church fetes and cake stalls but it also shows concern for a wide range of more important things.

There is an article, for example, about the St. Nicholas Institute for the Visually Handicapped in Penang, West Malaysia. This is a church-sponsored organisation which, among other things, uses a computer to produce books in Braille. There is an advert for a Traidcraft stall, selling articles from Third World countries in a way that ensures the producers get a fair share of the profits. There is a notice giving details of local recycling points for waste paper, bottle and aluminium cans.

Among the other material on the table at the back of the church are leaflets on Christian Aid, UNICEF and the work of the local Samaritans.

This church is clearly very well aware of the world outside its doors and all that needs to be done in it, but it is not just a centre for social work; it has a spiritual dimension too. A prayer leaflet offers suggestions for each day of the month for things to pray about concerning the church, the world and the local community.

The church is old, but on one of the altars is a beautiful modern embroidery with a very simple design showing a cross, a few ears of corn and a vine. It symbolises the bread and wine which Christians take as the body and blood of Christ, given for them, in the communion service. It is in this action, repeated week by week, that this church finds the spiritual power for its work in the world.

Colin Johnson

Note:
The rector of Leominster Priory, Prebendary M. W. Hooper writes:

'Some very exciting things happen here, and the church building has become very much the home of the community.'

The embroidered altar cloth mentioned in the text is illustrated in colour on the back cover of this booklet.

CHURCH BUILDINGS USED AS COMMUNITY BUILDINGS IN STANNINGLEY, LEEDS

The nineteenth century industrial village of Stanningley straddled approximately a mile of road between Bradford and Leeds and at one time had at least six 'sacred' buildings within that mile. As we approach the last decade of the twentieth century three of these are 'sacred' buildings. The oldest, the original Stanningley Methodist Preaching Place of 1796, has become St. John's Methodist. Next the Anglican Parish Church of St. Thomas, 148 years old; and the former Eleven Lane Ends Methodist Church, now Holy Spirit Roman Catholic Church. The other three buildings, one Anglican, one Methodist and one Baptist are now entirely secular commercial premises. Most of these churches had some connection with mills or engineering works which have disappeared. All three remaining sacred buildings in recent years have used their buildings to make a bridge between sacred and secular: Holy Spirit and St. John's with rooms for community use in the same buildings; the Anglican Parish Church with a succession of separate buildings: school, Memorial Institute and, latterly, Parish Hall.

Patchwork, an ecumenical project of the churches in Stanningley Parish, is an attempt to work out questions such as: can church buildings be used meaningfully by a whole community? Can we use them to express our experience of God in worship, and of God in our workday lives?

In co-operation with central government, local government, Kitson College of Technology Department of Printing, Heidleberg U.K., Agfa Gevaert and Mountleigh Properties, St. John's Methodist Church and St. Thomas' Parish Church have developed their buildings to provide the following. On the site of the parish hall adjacent to the parish church is the Patchwork Training Centre. This houses a print room, graphics room, work processing room and tutorial room. Here pupils from six schools come for one session a week for a curriculum involving printing skills, desk to publishing skills, design layout and paste-up and community journalism. Within this is an experiment to discover appropriate personal, social, moral and spiritual education.

The old St. John's building has been refurbish and extended to create the Stanningley Parish Community Education Centre with a small 'chapel in the midst' for approximately 40 people. In the community Education Centre voluntary groups from both churches, and other local community groups hold activities encouraging learning and growth, social intereaction and community service. The 'chapel in the midst' provides for the informal and intimate style of Methodist chapel worship.

The parish church is used for regular Anglican worship but also once a month for community services. At these services, groups using the Community Education Centre, the Patchwork Training Centre and other community groups such as partners in learning, are invited to contribute their weekday learning and experience to all age worship and celebration.

Alan Payne

Patchwork Training Centre with the parish church of St. Thomas in the foreground.

A CATHEDRAL IN POLAND

The country is Poland. It is a wet, chilly Saturday morning in Gdansk, the country's second city and an important and historic sea-port on the Baltic coast. The cathedral church in Oliwa, a western suburb of the city is packed to the doors to hear an organ recital. The organ is a very splendid one, with a great range of sound effects; and there are statues of trumpeters and other instrumentalists on its casing which come to life by mechanical means when the appropriate parts of a piece are reached. We listen to J. S. Bach's Toccata and Fugue in D minor, one of the most sensational pieces ever written for the organ; then there are more modern works, showing just what this organ can do.

All around, the crowd sits in quiet attention. Every age-group is represented. Many of the young people in their 'teens and early twenties wear Solidarity badges.

The music ends and over the loudspeakers comes an announcement, first in Polish, then in English, because British visitors are known to be present. A nun's voice explains that 'the concerts here are the contribution by the Catholic church to the creation and development of culture. May this concert encourage us contantly to reshape our inner lives so that we might come to know greater harmony through the grace of our Lord.' Then comes the invitation to all Christian people present to stand, face the altar and join in the Lord's Prayer. It seems that everyone does. There is a collection, a period of silence and then we all file out into the Baltic drizzle. Why were so many people there?

The reasons go deep into Polish history, especially recent history. For centuries Poland was an important sovereign state, influential in European affairs, with its own rich culture, its universities, some of the very first schools to be set up in all Eupope. But then it was divided amongst its more powerful neighbours: Czarist Russia seized eastern Poland, the Austro-Hungarian Empire the south, Prussia the west. These occupying powers, especially the Russians and Germans, tried to eradicate Polish culture, even the Polish language. All teaching in Polish and all Polish school textbooks were forbidden in the Russian and German territories. Yet, throughout this period, the Roman Catholic church, to which most Poles belonged, kept alive the sparks of Polish life and language. People went to church to remind themselves that they were Polish.

After the first world war, things seemed to be better for a time. The victorious allied powers, Britain, France and the United States, made Poland an independent country once again. Yet this freedom was short-lived. The rise of Hitler and the Nazis in Germany soon posed threats to Polish independence; and world war two started in September 1939 with the Nazi invasion of Poland. Simultaneously the Russian army moved in to eastern Poland and so the country was once more divided. There were five years of brutal occupation, a rising against the Germans which resulted in the complete destruction of Warsaw, Poland's historic capital. Gdansk was burned by the advancing Russian army at the end of the war because they saw it as a German, not a Polish city.

Then, in 1945 came peace, but the Russian army stayed in Poland and forced a Soviet-style communist government on what was supposed to be a free country. Only one party was allowed in parliament. Press, radio and television were controlled by the communist politicians. As is the way with communist governments, religion was outlawed. The communist government failed to manage Poland's economy successfully, so that daily queues for bread, meat and other necessities remained as facts of life for most people in Poland long after they had vanished elsewhere. People were queuing for bread and sausages in Gdansk that Saturday morning in 1989. Only with the decline of Stalinist governments in Rrussia and the eventual rise of Mr. Gorbachev was the Russian grip on Poland relaxed.

Throughout the war, the terrifying days of the occupation and the post-war years of communist domination, the Roman Catholic church kept alive Polish life and culture. It was disapproved of by the authorities and every possible obstacle was placed in its way; but so many Poles attended church that the communist authorities could never fully enforce their displeasure by banning it. Indeed, some officials were on-the-quiet Roman Catholics. The kind of thing that happened was that all church building and church repair was prohibited during normal working hours; so it was done at night. There was a least one case of a new church being built secretly in sections and erected overnight.

Working through Catholic charities, the church also found itself having to provide many of the welfare services which the state either would not or could not provide. Increasingly, alternative political ideas were developed and discussed in the relative safety of the churches. Sunday sermons all over Poland raised questions and put forward ideas about how Poland ought to be governed. The election of a Polish Pope and his visit to Poland raised the Roman Catholic hierarchy in Poland almost to the status of a political opposition. When the people's dissatisfaction with the communist party's ways of running the country became so great that the shipyard workers of Gdansk organised themselves into an illegal, free trade union, then into a major national political party, the Catholic hierarchy, with its great political expertise, was able to give the union's inexperienced leaders a great deal of unofficial advice.

So pressure on the failing communist government mounted; and in 1989 there were free elections in Poland, the first for fifty years, with a true choice of candidates and a real opposition party. In that historic year also, the official disapproval of the Catholic church was at last lifted. It would seem that people had crowded into the Gdansk cathedral that Saturday morning for many reasons. They felt, so they said, that their very Polishness was preserved and nourished in church; that here lay a real alternative to the dreary uniformity, the official incompetence, the frustrations and lack of freedom of life outside. Now, Poland is moving towards a wider freedom, towards full membership of the community of free European nations which is its right. Will people go to church when Poland is once more truly independent and when the church is no longer the stronghold of national identity and political freedom?

Will they go to church for God as they do today for Poland?

Patrick Bailey

Gdansk Cathedral, Poland, with decorative streamers.

47

TWO EVENTS IN THE CATHEDRAL OF ST. JOHN THE DIVINE, NEW YORK

1. THE FEAST OF THE RESURRECTION
Easter Day – 26th March 1989

"Cathedral of where . . .?" was the unpromising response of the New York cab driver. Easter Day, 1989, was brilliantly sunny with the Manhatten skyscrapers etched against the light. The Indian driver (having been shown our destination on our map) whisked us up Fifth Avenue, engaging us in conversation about his brother who had settled in the 'East End of London' and told us his own memories of living for several years in Brixton. Fifteen minutes later, we reached the vast building, now the second largest Christian structure in the world and at 10.55 a.m. we entered its dark impressive interior. We were each handed a printed twenty-four page Order of Service and we jostled our way to the north aisle where we joined the standing throng. Warmth and friendliness surrounded us; an unexpected smell of cooking drifted through a side door from the Cathedral Soup Kitchen. We waited for the procession to begin.

What a procession! Perhaps most significant was the number of clergy, both men and women from a wide range of racial backgrounds. One distinctive element in the worship at St. John the Divine is its use of traditions based on Catholic and Orthodox as well as on Anglican traditions. Another is a stress on the common heritage which Christians share with Jesus: where else would one have heard the Shema as the antiphon, or the first lesson read in Hebrew?

The first 'great moment' came after the Easter hymn 'Salve Feste Dies' with the Bishop making his last appearance at the cathedral before his retirement. The procession reached the west end turned and awaited the Bishop's entrance through the west door. His entrance announced with three echoing knocks on the great bronze doors. The trumpets sounded in fanfare and the procession moved forward, while all sang the Easter hymn, 'Jesus Christ is risen today, Alleluia'.

The next event of moment was the Bishop's sermon. This he began by walking the length of the cathedral addressing the congregation as individuals, using his button microphone, with his voice coming to us from all sides; this was the Bishop speaking to his flock as father and pastor, making his farewell; he disregarded the intrusive TV cameras and mounted the pulpit. Then followed his public affirmation of the gospel in his dynamic and challenging style; We were all made to link the Easter message with the all too evident needs of New York.

Thus, he said "good-bye", to thunderous and prolonged applause.

The Nicene Creed then fell into place as an affirmation of faith. The peace prayer and the prayer of the people, spoken in the numerous tongues of New York's inhabitants united all in the family of the Church, so that the peace was warmly exchanged: young and old, sick and well, friends and strangers, all present at 'the sacred' banquet the Eucharist, even if not partaking of it.

Bill Greenwood

"Cathedral Nights" . . . presents

ENVIRONMENT & RELIGIOUS LIFE

The crisis of the environment presents an unmistakable spiritual challenge. To save our planet, our lives must change. We know such work must begin within. But many of us are seeking direction and support for our efforts.

On each Tuesday in October, at 7pm, we will explore practical ways to revere and care for the Earth: the prayers we offer and the products we buy, private acts in solitude and citizen action in solidarity.

Through worship, formal presentations, informal discussions, music and eucharist, we will work to "receive the earth", God's sacred Creation, more deeply into our hearts, habits and households.

October 3 — **Nature and the Word**
...ings of prose and poetry evoke the beauty of ...on and lead us to share experiences of how ... has helped awaken and support our ...s life. **William Bryant Logan & readers.**

...er 10 — **Beholding and Behaving**
...ve cultivate mind and senses to be more ...mmunion with nature, even in the city? ...habits can we change to live ...ally sound lives? **Paul Gorman &**

October 17 — **Earth Judec Stor**
The plight of the Earth, what ...tion, calls all people of faith ... What understandings must ... reaffirmed, revised; must a ... **Dean James Parks Morto**

October 24 — **"Ir ir**
Do we believe in the pov ... and when, specifically, ... the Earth? **The Rev. I**

October 31
Halloween as Hallow ... collaborate in a fina' ... supreme mystery.

The Cathedral Church of St. John the Divine • Amsterdam Avenue at 112th Street • New York City, NY • 1989

Some activities at the Cathedral of St. John the Divine,
New York, U.S.A.

2. AIDS: AN INTER-FAITH SERVICE.

A Service of Hope – Sunday, 5th November 1989

Events in the USA start very promptly. This should be no exception, but there are apologies over the cathedral loudspeaker system. Unexpectedly, the sub-way is not running betwen 96 and 124 Streets and this is causing chaos and delays. The service will have to start later than planned.

The interior of the cathedral is dimly lit; the last of the light outside glows against the nave windows. Every member of the already huge congregation is given a candle, unlit so far.

At last the service starts and the procession enters. The organ prelude is very moving; loud, discordant, wild. The procession is colourful; it includes people of many different ethnic groups and different religions; the new Bishop of New York brings up the rear. He wears his cope and mitre and carries his pastoral staff.

Everyone joins in 'Immortal, invisible, God only wise', and there are prayers and readings. The Jewish shema is read in Hebrew and the OM (a Hindu name for God) is intoned by a Hindu. The Addicts' Rehabilitation Centre Gospel Choir sings. One powerful male voice pleads: "Turn us away from drugs".

Towards the end of the service the candles are lit in memory of those who have died from AIDS. All then move with lighted candles to the cathedral's AIDS Memorial and stand there in silent prayer. I find this service an almost unbearably moving experience.

Brenda Lealman

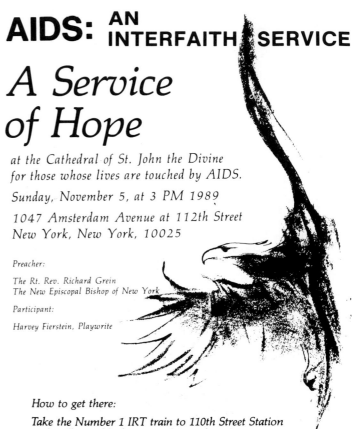

AIDS: AN INTERFAITH SERVICE

A Service of Hope

at the Cathedral of St. John the Divine for those whose lives are touched by AIDS.

Sunday, November 5, at 3 PM 1989

1047 Amsterdam Avenue at 112th Street New York, New York, 10025

Preacher:

*The Rt. Rev. Richard Grein
The New Episcopal Bishop of New York*

Participant:

Harvey Fierstein, Playwrite

How to get there:

Take the Number 1 IRT train to 110th Street Station and walk one block east to Amsterdam Avenue.

CHRISTIAN BUILDINGS
AROUND
THE WORLD

STAVE CHURCH SOGNEFJIORD NORWAY

NOTRE DAME DE HAUT.

RUSSIAN ORTHODOX CHURCH

HIROSHIMA PEACE CHURCH . JAPAN

COPTIC ORTHODOX CATHEDRAL OF ST MARKS . CAIRO EGYPT.

A CATHEDRAL IN THE CANADIAN ARTIC

The cold is sharp, intense. I am on my way to the arctic, to a settlement well on the way to the north pole. I have a few hours to wait for my connecting flight in Iqaluit. Snow; treeless landscape; piercingly blue sea; cabin-like houses; slippery tracks through the snow . . . I am determined to pay a quick visit to the Cathedral of St. Jude.

A cathedral like an igloo

There is no mistaking Iqaluit Cathedral. It is a white building shaped like an igloo or, more correctly, an igluviga or snow house. Until very recent years, the Inuit or Eskimos lived in snow houses in winter but nowadays they are usually only built when the Eskimos are away hunting for several days.

The cathedral in Iqaluit.

Inside

Wooden steps lead up to the entrance to the cathedral. The main body of the cathedral is windowless. Its plan is typically Anglican: altar in front, reading desk at the side and benches in front. Interestingly, however, many of the furnishings have been made by members of the congregation and they depict an Eskimo way of life which is quickly disappearing. The pulpit is made out of a sledge or kamotik, standing in an upright position. The communion rails are sledges standing on their sides. The kneelers are made from seal skin and the hymn board is shaped like a snow shovel. Near to the pulpit stands a fish spear. The altar is a memorial to Bishop Fleming, the first bishop of the diocese of the arctic, and was given by his wife. Bishop Fleming's crozier or staff stands in the cathedral. It is made of aluminium and at the neck is a collar made of the minerals which are found in north-west Canada: gold, silver, copper, lead and zinc.

Uses

The cathedral is less than twenty years old. Since last century Christianity has spread widely amongst the Inuit. Now, about 250 Eskimo families and about 150 others are members of Iqaluit Cathedral congregation. Services are held every Sunday at 10.00 a.m. in English, at 11.00 a.m. and 7.00 p.m. in Eskimo or in Inuktitut. There is a very active Eskimo Sunday school and the cathedral is much involved with the young people of Iqaluit. Every night of the week except during the brief summer period there is something going on either at the cathedral or the parish hall. Later, I was to meet the dean of the cathedral and some of the Christians who attend it. I was to have many fascinating conversations with Eskimos about how they view the world and about their religion. Just now, however, I leave the cathedral and make my way, rather gingerly, through the snow and ice back to the airport. Two dark little eyes peer at me from the hood of a parka: Inuit women carry babies about in their hooded parkas. The wind stings my face.

Brenda Lealman

Inuit priest setting out to visit his parishioners over the artic snow.

Inuktitut Language.

A VILLAGE CHURCH ON THE ISLAND OF ST. HELENA

Arriving

We arrived as Napoleon did. There is no other way to arrive. Our ship, which brought us on the 15-day journey from England, anchored in the harbour. A little boat carried us from ship to shore and we stepped on to the Island of St. Helena.

The little colonial capital huddles in a steep valley running down to the sea. The cliffs and rocks tower above us as we walk in the sunshine and heat of a tropical day. Our island is in the middle of the Atlantic Ocean, far from any land, but the Union Jack still flies from the castle flagpole. The island has an English Governor, representing the Queen. English is the only language spoken though the islanders are a brown people of very mixed race. Because of its isolation, Napoleon was brought here as a prisoner after the Battle of Waterloo and died on the island after six years of exile.

The Briars

Now we are hot and tired. We have walked up the steep road leading from the valley. Below us the ocean sparkles and the capital basks in the afternoon sun. We have come to the first village in the hills above the town. It is called 'The Briars' and the biggest house in the village was the first of Napoleon's two prisons on St. Helena. But here on our left, sandwiched between the narrow village road and the rocky hillside, is the little church of 'St. Mary-The-Briars'.

St. Mary's

The tiny church is painted white and shines brightly in the tropical sun. It has only just been rebuilt by the villagers. It was a one-roomed cottage, just like the small old cottages of the village and though there are only 100 people in the village, nearly all are Anglicans and the old church was too small!

Now its windows have coloured glass. A new tin roof is painted. There is a little vestry added at the side. It is the work of the St. Helenians in the village.

The blocks for rebuilding the walls were made locally and a village man and his son put them in place. All the village men came to help mix concrete for the floor. The newly polished benches, the sanctuary rail, and the cross on the roof reflect the local skill in woodworking. The recent work has not changed the feel of the chapel. It is homely, domestic, in the style of the village cottages and it is a part of village life.

The priest comes regularly from the capital and there are weekly services. The village Sunday school and the confirmation classes are held here. Hazel, the 'chapelwarden' for St. Mary's, has singing practices in the evenings, using the small electric organ the villagers bought themselves. It was the place too for rehearsals for village shows.

Glory from the humble

St. Helena is a very isolated community. There are no 'planes. The ship calls only every two months. Most of the villagers of the Briars have never seen the traffic lights, shopping centres and motorways of the 'big world'. As we leave St. Mary's Church and walk through the blazing reds and purples of the village's bougainvillea, Mr. Williams has started to ring the new bell. This was a gift from England. The island's cable station is in the Briars and the villagers who work for Cable and Wireless put it up on the roof. As we walk away with the bell echoing across the hillsides, we know that the praises and prayers of that simple homely village are as lovely to God as those of the grandest cathedrals of the world away across the oceans.

Michael Houghton

THE CATHEDRAL CHURCH OF ST. JOHN THE DIVINE, NEW YORK

This is the mental picture I had brought with me from England to New York: no lone traveller on the sub-way survives for more than two stations. But, I figured, the challenge was worth it. I plotted my route along the sub-way's grid system and put my dollar token in the turnstyle. On to the platform. Train to 110 Street Cathedral Parkway. A short walk along 110 Street, up Amsterdam Avenue, and I was facing the second largest Christian church in the world (St. Peter's Rome, has an area of 227,069 square feet and the Cathedral of St. John the Divine has an area in square feet of 121,000).

The cathedral's huge west front looms over the road. It is in French Gothic style and the two west towers are yet to be built. (The foundation stone of the cathedral was laid in 1892 and the building is still unfinished.) The magnificent stone carving on the west front are based on scenes from the Christian Bible.

I enter through one of the five west doors and find myself in the space immediately inside the west end or narthex, entrance hall or place of preparation: time to slow down and become quiet before entering the main part of the building.

Mysterious
The nave is dim and mysterious. The pillars rise up for one hundred feet and then form the vaulted ceiling.

I revel in the semi-darkness, the glow of the jewel-like windows along the nave. Perhaps what excites me most about the cathedral is its celebration of God at work in the whole of creation. To my left is a bay in the outermost north aisle which is called the Sports Bay. The window above the bay's altar shows bowling, swimming, skating, car racing, boxing, ice hockey, football, baseball, tennis, fencing and many other games. Another bay has a shrine to sacred geometry (number systems and mathematics at the root of architecture). One bay has an earth shrine: a 2,000 pound natural crystal cluster which was found at Hot Springs, Arkansas. There is also a huge ammonite fossil. God in creation. Medicine is also celebrated with a window to Hippocrates, "the father of medicine".

Granite
At the east end of the cathedral is the great choir and the high altar. Behind the altar are eight giant granite columns. Their effect is overwhelming. So is that of the whole choir; many different kinds of marble, stone and tile help to give the impression of the vision of the New Jerusalem recorded in the last book of the Bible, the Revelation to St. John the Divine. There are many subtle and different colours here and behind all is the flashing brilliance of the great windows.

Jewish candlesticks burning
One of the most beautiful objects in the choir are the menorah candlesticks. These are two massive seven-branched candle holders flanking the high altar. Each is made of bronze overlaid with gold and weighs more than a ton. The candle holders were given to the cathedral by a Jewish man who was deeply moved by the Bishop of New York's protests against the persecutions of Jews in Russia before the Russian Revolution early this century. The candles burn constantly: as memorials to the millions of Jews who perished in the holocaust in the Second World War; as signs of the debt which Christians owe to Jews; as reminders of the consequences of racial and religious narrowmindedness.

Full of life
This is a living, dynamic cathedral. Lively and often unusual worship with drama and dancing takes place here. There is worship with people of faiths other than Christianity; there are pop concerts, classical music concerts; involvement with some of the poorest people in New York; art exhibitions; a Listening Room for a ministry to anyone in need.

Brenda Lealman

Saccidananda Ashram, South India.

A CHRISTIAN CHURCH IN SOUTH INDIA

In India, temples close in the heat of the day; it is the siesta time for the gods and goddesses. It is siesta time, too, for human beings. Mad dogs and English people, however, do not readily abandon the streets of India and I have no intention of doing so. I leave the temple with the burning hot flag-stones in its court yard, and hire a motor rickshaw. Away we roar. Temple monkeys and street vendors eye us with some interest. We career madly around the narrow streets and finally end up at Trichy (Tiruchchirappalli, Tamil Nadu, South India) bus station. From here I am taking a bus south, to Tannirpali and Saccidananda Ashram (an ashram is a religious community). It is a dusty country bus with wooden seats: full of people, grinning brown faces and huge brown eyes. How will I know when to get off? Will anyone know of the religious community which I am going to visit? . . . No need to worry. The whole bus is keen to point out at which lane end I have to get off the bus. "Just down there," they cry.

Peace
I set off down the track through banana, papaya and coconut groves. I am heading into the 'forest of peace' (Shanti Vanam). At the ashram I am warmly and courteously welcome. The small hut with a straw roof which I am given has next to nothing in it – just a stone slab to sleep on. The 'bathroom' is a dark little out-house with a cold water tap in it and a frog. But that is not the point. I have come here for peace and reflection. And, peace is here. Peace is even more deeply present when I go to my own little meditation hermitage deep beneath the banana trees in the lush vegetation near to the river.

Meditation
An ashram in India means a religious community or more precisely, the dwelling place of a guru or spiritual teacher who leads people to God. Ashrams are usually Hindu and the guru can be any one of hundreds of holy persons, almost invariably although not always, a living person. The ashram I am staying in is different in so far as it is Christian and Christ is the guru. The leader of the community is a Catholic Benedictine called Father Bede Griffiths. He is

Meditation hut.

very old, very wise, and his beautiful and calm face radiates peace. He spends most of his time in prayer and meditation but also finds time to talk to every one of his visitors at least once each week.

Christian church like a Hindu temple

This is Christianity in a Hindu land and this is reflected in the church buildings and in the worship. It is all very different from Christianity and its buildings in western Europe.

The small chapel is built in the style of a Siva temple. It has a small dark inner sanctuary and there is an inverted lotus for an altar. There are little oil lights in triangular niches in the wall. Over the door of the sanctuary there is an inscription in the Hindu sacred language, Sanskrit: "Lord of the World, you alone are the Supreme being. There is no other." This is a quotation from one of the Hindu sacred books.

Between the inner and outer courts of the chapel or temple stands the Christian cross enclosed in a circle. At the centre of the cross is the Hindu word OM. The gateway to the whole 'temple' area has an elaborate carving on top of it. It is done in the tradition of the brightly coloured folk art of the surrounding villages. It represents the Hindu ideas of a three-sided God: God as creator, preserver, and destroyer of evil. It leads us towards the experience or awareness (*cit*) of the absolute (*sat*) which is bliss (*ananda*). Hence the full name of the ashram: Saccidananda Ashram. Worship, too, is deeply influenced by Hinduism. There are three prayer meetings a day: early in the morning, at noon, and in the evening. There are readings from Christian and from Hindu Scriptures. There are Sanskrit chants and hymns, and there is the ceremony of light (*arati*), and the taking of ashes (marked on the forehead).

Interfaith meetings

I am privileged to be able to attend some inter-faith meetings at the Saccidananda Ashram. This is India and it is worth thinking about what Mahatma Gandhi, a Hindu, said "I do not want my house to be walled in on all sides and my windows to be stuffed. I want the culture of all lands to be blown about my house as freely as possible because I refuse to be blown off my feet by any of them." Some Christian buildings reflect such feelings; Saccidananda Ashram does. It also assets that prayer, silence and contemplation are near the heart of Christianity.

Brenda Lealman

Small Christian shrines built like Hindu shrines.

Eating a simple meal in the ashram.

CHURCHES IN BURMA

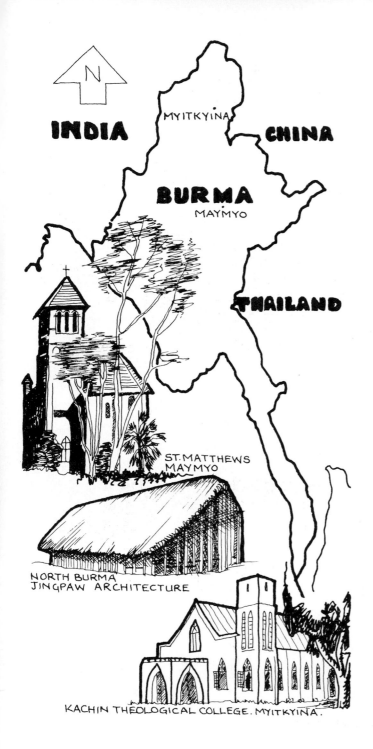

INDIA
CHINA
MYITKYINA
BURMA
MAYMYO
THAILAND

ST. MATTHEWS
MAYMYO

NORTH BURMA
JINGPAW ARCHITECTURE

KACHIN THEOLOGICAL COLLEGE. MYITKYINA.

In Burma, churches who can afford it, construct their buildings out of bricks, cement and zinc. Many buildings are much simpler, made out of wooden poles, bamboos and thatch. The village churches are like that.

Most churches are built in the shape of a cross. They are used for worship, preaching, teaching, weddings and dramatisations.

Many churches have one or two choir groups. Children only occasionally join in adult worship; they have junior church.

There are Roman Catholic and Protestant churches and the latter worship very much like non-conformist churches in England.

Sabaw Sinwa Naw

Note:
Burma is a mainly Buddhist country on the borders of India. Most Christians are found amongst the tribal peoples who live in the hills along Burma's borders. They feel that the Buddhists are the ruling group in Burma.

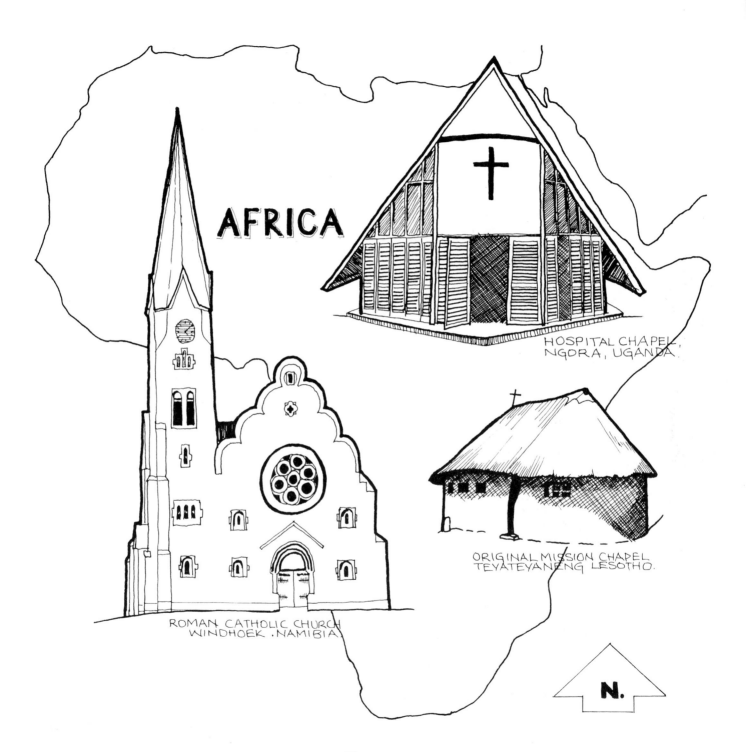

AFRICA

HOSPITAL CHAPEL, NGORA, UGANDA.

ORIGINAL MISSION CHAPEL, TEYATEYANENG LESOTHO.

ROMAN CATHOLIC CHURCH WINDHOEK .NAMIBIA.

N.

PAPUA NEW GUINEA
CHURCH OF LOCAL MATERIAL

BRAZIL
18TH CENTURY ROMAN CATHOLIC CHURCH RIO DE JANEIRO.

AUSTRALIA
SIMPLE STONE SALVATION ARMY HALL URALLA NEW SOUTH WALES.

PAPUA NEW GUINEA

AUSTRALIA

URALLA

PACIFIC OCEAN.

BRAZIL.

0°

RIO DE JANEIRO·   23.5°S

N.

AUSTRALASIA , SOUTH AMERICA